Air Fryer Cookbook for Healthy Family Meals

The Best and Most Loved Quick and Easy Recipes for Everyday Cooking on a Budget

Written By

Linda Rea

Legal & Disclaimer

The information contained in this book and its contents is not designed to replace or take the place of any form of medical or professional advice; and is not meant to replace the need for independent medical, financial, legal or other professional advice or services, as may be required. The content and information in this book has been provided for educational and entertainment purposes only.

The content and information contained in this book have been compiled from sources deemed reliable, and it is accurate to the best of the Author's knowledge, information, and belief. However, the author cannot guarantee its accuracy and validity and cannot be held liable for any errors and/or omissions. Further, changes are periodically made to this book as and when needed. Where appropriate and/or necessary, you must consult a professional (including but not limited to your doctor, attorney, financial advisor or such other professional advisor) before using any of the suggested remedies, techniques, or information in this book.

Upon using the contents and information contained in this book, you agree to hold harmless the Author from and against any damages, costs, and expenses, including any legal fees potentially resulting from the application of any of the information provided by this book. This disclaimer applies to any loss, damages or injury caused by the use and application, whether directly or indirectly, of any advice or information presented, whether for breach of contract, tort, negligence, personal injury, criminal intent, or under any other cause of action.

You agree to accept all risks of using the information presented inside this book.

You agree that by continuing to read this book, where appropriate and/or necessary, you shall consult a professional (including but not limited to your doctor, attorney, or financial advisor or such other advisor as needed) before using any of the suggested remedies, techniques, or information in this book.

Table of Contents

Breaded mushrooms 55

Greek Meatballs with Feta 57

Lemon sole and swiss chard 59

Prawn Burgers 61

Sardine Cakes 63

Mahi-mahi And Broccoli Cakes 65

Tuna Au Gratin With Herbs 67

Shrimp And Pine Nuts Mix 69

Garlic tarragon buttered salmon 71

Crumbed fish fillets with tarragon 73

Smoked and creamed white fish 75

Fish and cauliflower cakes 77

Grilled salmon with butter and wine 79

Mouth Watering Pork Tenderloin with Bell Pepper 81

Ground Beef 83

Rolled Up Tender Beef 85

& GREEN 87

Cinnamon butternut squash fries 89

Cheesy artichokes 91

Paprika tomatoes 93

Avocado and tomato salad 95

Sesame broccoli mix 97

Cabbage sauté 99

Tomatoes and kidney beans 101

Glazed mushrooms 103

Balsamic zucchini slices 105

INTRODUCTION

Can I cook my 'lean and green' dishes using

an Air Fryer?

The answer is **YES,** absolutely.

If you already own (or you are thinking of buying) an **Air Fryer** you will have in your hands all the tools that will guarantee you top results. You can use your Air Fryer to cook all your *'lean and green'* dishes from this cookbook in a quick and easy way, without compromising on taste and while staying within budget!

As you might already know, an air fryer is a small type of oven. It is an innovative countertop kitchen gadget that fries or cook's food by circulating hot air via convection current. The air fryer has a heating ring that produces hot air. There is also a mechanical fan that circulates the hot air all over the food at high speed. This hot air cook or fries the food to give the same crispy product as the oil fried variety. The difference between air frying and oil frying is that while oil frying involves immersion of the food into the hot oil to cook, the air fryer doesn't. It means that you can achieve the same cooking results as in oil frying but with little to no oil.

The air fryer works great for foods like roasted vegetables, especially roasted garlic, bacon, whole chicken, wings, eggs, meat, and fish. Most air fryers come with timers and temperature adjustments to make for more precise cooking. There is an opening at the top that takes in air, heated up by the heating rings, and subsequently blown over the food, thereby efficiently cooking them. A cooking basket also sits on top of a drip tray inside which the food is cooked. This basket needs to be shaken frequently to ensure even mixing of oil and a better cooking result. While most models have agitators that initiate this shaking at regular intervals, most others do not, and the shaking should be done manually.

Since air fryers don't require as much oil as oil frying does, they are generally considered healthier. An air fryer reduces the oil content of food to nearly 80% less than oil frying. It is because the food does not absorb as much oil as with oil frying. However, this difference has led to arguments about the taste of air fried food compared to the oil fried variety. Since oil adds more flavor to fried food as it is being absorbed, it comes as no surprise if an air fried food tastes slightly different from oil fried ones. An excellent example is French fries that may taste a lot different when air fried than the usual oil fried delicacy. Chicken, however, turns out pretty great whether sprinkled with oil or not before air frying.

Moreover, spraying the food with oil before air frying gives it an added crispiness compared to the one that was not sprinkled before air frying. Oil on its own is also one of the essential macronutrients and will come in handy in the right proportion.

There are many heart friendly oils out there, which you can spread over your food before air frying to achieve that fabulous taste. These oils can be used to sprinkle your food before air frying to maintain a healthier diet. Just like most innovative appliances, the air fryer might come with an initial dread on how to use it effectively. Once mastered, the art of air frying is what many people find themselves resorting to more often than not. Even though air frying is a convenient hands-off cooking method, using the air fryer is more than just turning on the device and leaving your kitchen.

What are the benefits of an Air Fryer?

As you are aware, an air fryer is a great appliance to have in your kitchen. Not only does it save on the time taken to cook, but it also produces healthy meals. It's worthwhile looking at some of the health benefits provided by it.

- Healthy foods

The air fryer is quite popular, owing to producing healthy meals. It reduces oils and fats, thereby making the result relatively healthy. The same cannot be said about standard cooking techniques where you must add in lots of oils and fats. These can adversely affect your health and be the reason for obesity and illnesses. Therefore, an air fryer is best suited for improving their health by making changes in their cooking habits.

- Time

The time crunch is one of the most significant issues people face today and age, as everybody is preoccupied with one thing or another. The air fryer effectively solves this problem, as you can prepare foods within a short period. It works by cutting down on 20% of the time taken to cook foods the traditional way. This feature comes in handy for many people, including working professionals, students, and the elderly. If you are always short of time, then it is best to invest in an air fryer as soon as you get a chance.

- Usage

The air fryer is extremely easy to use and can be used by just about anyone. The machine is supplied with a manual that can be used to operate the appliance. The manual will also provide you with the right temperatures and times to cook different meals. With time, you will know the exact measures and be able to cook meals much faster. However, it will take a certain level of trial and error to stumble upon the right temperatures and times until you get used to using it. Remember, your ideas center around traditional cooking.

- Effort required

The air fryer is designed to be a very efficient machine that pretty much works by itself. It means that you don't have to put in too much effort to operate it. You just have to prepare the ingredients and add them to the appliance, and it will take it from there. You don't have to sauté, season, cover or keep an eye on the foods you place into the oven. All these steps are eliminated, thereby reducing both your effort and time taken to cook a meal. It makes it ideal for all those who are usually too lazy to cook up a meal and prefer takeout.

- Nutritional content

An air fryer helps maintain food's nutritional value. Cooking foods at higher temperatures can cause nutritional value to deplete. This issue is solved with an air fryer as it retains the nutritional content of foods placed into it.

- Cost of cooking

The air fryer helps in cutting down on the overall costs of cooking. It cuts down on the use of oils and fats, thereby reducing the overall costs of providing your family with food. Another advantage of cooking with an air fryer is that it tends to expand the food item, thereby decreasing the quantity required to cook a meal, reducing cooking costs. You will be surprised by the reduction in your budget and overall cooking costs.

- Variety in cooking

Throwing parties and cooking big meals will now be quite easy thanks to the air fryer's multitasking ability. One of the most advantages of using an air fryer is that it can be used for many different cooking purposes. Right from roasting to frying to baking, the air fryer can be put to many uses. You can also use it to grill foods, making it a truly versatile appliance to have in your kitchen. What's more, you will have the choice of cooking several dishes at the same time by using the separator provided with the fryer.

- Maintaining the fryer

It is easy to maintain the air fryer, as you do not have to do too much to stay clean. You can eliminate the need to clean several appliances and get away with cleaning, just one that servings many purposes. The machine is easy to clean from the outside. The basket and catching utensil are dishwasher friendly.

- Cost saving

The air fryer is quite cheap, price wise, considering the utility that it can provide. You don't need to buy different appliances like an oven, a grill, a chip fryer, etc. It can be done through the air fryer alone. Think of it as a onetime investment that is sure to last you a lifetime if taken care of following manufacturer instructions. Always read these, as the maintenance of each fryer will differ.

These descriptions show the different benefits of using air fryer. Each one of these contributes towards making it an ideal appliance to have in your kitchen.

Any tips on using Air Fryer?

An air fryer is a little device that has rapidly grown in popularity in the last few years. It is supposed to help you bake food. Some people call them air fryer ovens. You may remember when you saw your first Indian dish inspired by food fried in oil. Now, it's time to take you on a tour of the world and in a healthier way!

In the last few years, air fryers have become more and more popular. A lot of websites and blogs are now making them out to be the new microwave oven or rice cooker. The fine folks at Amana, pioneers in air fryers, sent me one of their most hot selling models.

Frying has become a bad word lately. As a result, we try to cut down on it in as many of our recipes as possible. Fortunately, air fryers are a great way to make food taste like it's been fried when it hasn't. So, here are some tips on cooking with air fryers:

Air fryers are available in multiple sizes. Look for one that fits the amount of food you want to make. Some air fryers are small enough that you would only use them for a snack or a single person. Others could make enough food for a whole family. There's also a market for commercial sized air fryers, and they're quite large. They could make enough food for a dozen people easily. They're also versatile in that they can be used for baking and as steamers.

Your new air fryer comes with a lot of accessories. You don't need to worry too much about them at the moment. Here are a few tips.

These are the top 10 tips on
Using Air Fryer

1. No matter what your air fryer comes with, you'll also need a pan and a spatula. The pan is for use as a defroster and a catch-all for when you take out the food. The spatula is to get food out of the air fryer. Remember that the food comes out very hot, so use caution.

2. Look at the shape of your air fryer. It may be a square or a circle. You can do a lot of things to a square air fryer, but few to a circle one. Look at your recipe and decide what you want to use it for.

3. The air fryer's controls are arguably the most important part. The air fryer has a lot of temperature controls that are quite precise. Unlike a microwave oven, an air fryer can give you a wide range of temperatures. You can cook things at really low temperatures, and you can cook things at incredibly hot temperatures that you couldn't use otherwise. Of course, you can also use it at the default temperature. Use the recommendations for your model in the instruction manual to help figure out which temperature is best for your needs.

4. You can make very unique recipes using the air fryer. The temperature and the food you use set the tone of the meal. The temperature you want to use should depend mostly on the type of food you're making, or even how you want it to come out. Low temperature cooking is helpful when you want to cook things slowly. You also want foods with a lot of moisture to be cooked at a high temperature because they cook through faster. You can make dishes with vegetables and meats evenly. You can also make quick breads since they would take less time and the other ingredients are easier to get.

5. Air fryers are very inexpensive. No matter what your budget is, there is an air fryer that fits it. They're mainly used for snacks. However, you can use the air fryer for other recipes if you want. They're a great alternative to the waffle iron, and you can cook a wide range of foods with them.

6. There are different components to an air fryer, and you can use each of them for different purposes. The top is traditionally used for eggs and for steaming. The middle can be used for both frying foods and steaming them. The bottom is typically for fries and other fried foods.

7. Air fryers are very versatile. It's hard to find a recipe that can't be used in an air fryer. It's possible to make chicken legs, wings, and even drumsticks. You can even make foods with breading. People can even make grills and pizzas in air fryers.

8. If you're looking for the best air fryer, you can't go wrong with a Norpro. This is a great air fryer that is affordable and very easy to use. It has multiple functions and will work in no time.

9. Most air fryers have a filter. You need to make sure you always keep the filter cleaned. As much as you don't want to clean your air fryer, you have to clean the filter. This is very important because all the cooking oil is retained in the filter.

10. There are different types of air fryers. The ones that are made of glass and stainless steel are the most expensive. They're also more attractive. There are the ones that are made of plastic. Finally, there are the ones that are made from non-stick surfaces. These are the cheapest and also the most commonly sold air fryers.

Now you have in your hands all the information needed to safely proceed toward your OPTAVIA lifelong transformation to increase your Health, your Confidence and your Vitality. Using your Air Fryer will also guarantee you delicious and time effective recipes that will help you integrate the foundational Habits of Health into your everyday routine. By incorporating the Habits of Health into your new lifestyle, you will be able to take your first steps towards the life you wish for. You will feel restored, more confident and your energy levels will be up. Enjoy life to the fullest!

LEAN

Tabasco shrimp

Preparation time: 10 minutes

Cooking time: 10 minutes

Servings: 4

Ingredients:

- 1-pound shrimp, peeled and deveined
- 1 teaspoon red pepper flakes
- 2 tablespoon olive oil
- 1 teaspoon tabasco sauce
- 2 tablespoons water
- 1 teaspoon oregano, dried
- Salt and black pepper to the taste
- ½ teaspoon parsley, dried
- ½ teaspoon smoked paprika

Directions:

1. In a bowl, mix oil with water, tabasco sauce, pepper flakes, oregano, parsley, salt, pepper, paprika and shrimp and toss well to coat.

2. Transfer shrimp to your preheated air fryer at 370° f and cook for 10 minutes shaking the fryer once.

3. Divide shrimp on plates and serve with a side salad.

4. Enjoy!

Nutrition: calories 200, fat 5, fiber 6, carbs 13, protein 8

Stuffed calamari

Preparation time: 10 minutes

Cooking time: 25 minutes

Servings: 4

Ingredients:

- 4 big calamari, tentacles separated and chopped, and tubes reserved

- 2 tablespoons parsley, chopped

- 5 ounces kale, chopped

- 2 garlic cloves, minced

- 1 red bell pepper, chopped

- 1 tablespoon olive oil

- 2 ounces canned tomato puree

- 1 yellow onion, chopped

- Salt and black pepper to the taste

Directions:

1. Heat the pan with the oil over medium heat, add onion and garlic, stir and cook for 2 minutes.

2. Add bell pepper, tomato puree, calamari tentacles, kale, salt and pepper, stir, cook for 10 minutes and take off heat. Stir and cook for 3 minutes.

3. Stuff calamari tubes with this mix, secure with toothpicks, put in your air fryer and cook at 360 ° f for 20 minutes.

4. Divide calamari on plates, sprinkle parsley all over and serve.

5. Enjoy!

Nutrition: calories 322, fat 10, fiber 14, carbs 14, protein 22

Snapper fillets and veggies

Preparation time: 10 minutes

Cooking time: 14 minutes

Servings: 2

Ingredients:

- 2 red snapper fillets, boneless

- 1 tablespoon olive oil

- ½ cup red bell pepper, chopped

- ½ cup green bell pepper, chopped

- ½ cup leeks, chopped

- Salt and black pepper to the taste

- 1 teaspoon tarragon, dried

- A splash of white wine

Directions:

1. Put a hot proof dish that fits your air fryer, mix fish fillets with salt, pepper, oil, green bell pepper, red bell pepper, leeks, tarragon and wine.

2. Toss well everything, introduce in preheated air fryer at 350° f and cook for 14 minutes, flipping fish fillets halfway.

3. Divide fish and veggies on plates and serve warm.

4. Enjoy!

Nutrition: calories 300, fat 12, fiber 8, carbs 29, protein 12

Jumbo Shrimp

Preparation Time: 5 minutes

Cooking Time: 10 Minutes

Servings: 4

Ingredients:

- 12 jumbo shrimps
- ½ tsp. garlic salt
- ¼ tsp. freshly cracked mixed peppercorns

For the Sauce:

- 1 tsp. Dijon mustard
- 4 tbsp. mayonnaise
- 1 tsp. lemon zest
- 1 tsp. chipotle powder
- ½ tsp. cumin powder

Directions:

1. Dust garlic salt over the shrimp and coat with the cracked peppercorns.
2. Fry the shrimp in the cooking basket at 395degreesF for 5 minutes.
3. Turn the shrimp over and allow to cook for a further 2 minutes.

4. In the meantime, mix together all ingredients for the sauce with a whisk.

5. Serve over the shrimp.

Nutrition: Calories: 148 Fat: 4g Carbs: 2g Protein: 24g

Greek style Monkfish With Vegetables

Preparation Time: 10 minutes

Cooking Time: 20 Minutes

Servings: 2

Ingredients:

- 2 teaspoons olive oil

- 1 cup celery, sliced

- 2 bell peppers, sliced

- 1 teaspoon dried thyme

- 1/2 teaspoon dried marjoram

- 1/2 teaspoon dried rosemary

- 2 monkfish fillets

- 1 tablespoon soy sauce

- 2 tablespoons lime juice

- Coarse salt

- Ground black pepper, to taste

- 1 teaspoon cayenne pepper

- 1/2 cup pitted and sliced Kalamata olives

Directions:

1. Heat the olive oil for minute. Once hot, sauté the celery and peppers until tender, about 4 minutes.

2. Sprinkle with thyme, marjoram, and rosemary and set aside.

3. Toss the fish fillets with the soy sauce, lime juice, salt, black pepper, and cayenne pepper.

4. Position fish fillets in a lightly greased cooking basket and bake at 390° F for 8 minutes.

5. Turn them over, add the olives, and cook an additional 4 minutes. Serve with the sautéed vegetables on the side. Bon appétit!

Nutrition: Calories: 210 Fat: 13g Carbs: 9g Protein: 16g

Greek style Grilled Scallops

Preparation Time: 2 hours

Cooking Time: 15 minutes

Servings:3

Ingredients:

- ¼ cup 0% fat Greek yogurt

- A pinch of saffron threads

- 1 ½ teaspoons rice vinegar

- Salt and pepper to taste

- 12 large sea scallops

- 2 tablespoons olive oil

Directions:

1. Arrange all ingredients in a Ziploc and allow the scallops to marinate in the fridge for at least 2 hours.

2. Preheat the air fryer at 3900°F.

3. Place the grill pan accessory in the air fryer.

4. Grill the scallops for 15 minutes.

5. Serve on bread and drizzle with more olive oil if desired.

Nutrition: Calories: 392 Fat: 29g Carbs: 5g Protein: 29g

Savory Chicken Burgers

Preparation Time: 10 minutes

Cooking time: 10 minutes

Servings: 4

Ingredients:

- 1 lb. ground chicken

- ½ onion, chopped

- 2 garlic cloves, chopped

- 1 egg, beaten

- ½ cup whole wheat breadcrumbs

- ½ tbsp ground cumin

- ½ tbsp paprika

- ½ tbsp cilantro seeds, crushed

- Salt and black pepper to taste

Directions:

1. In a bowl, mix chicken, onion, garlic, egg, breadcrumbs, cumin, paprika, cilantro, salt, and black pepper, with hands; shape into 4 patties.

2. Grease the air fryer with oil and arrange the patties inside. Do not layer them. Cook in batches if needed.

3. Cook for 10 minutes at 380° F, turning once halfway through.

Nutrition: Calories: 250 Fat: 13g Carbs: 5g Protein: 26g

Chicken Tenders with Tarragon

Preparation Time: 10 minutes

Cooking time: 12 minutes

Servings: 2

Ingredients:

- 2 chicken tenders

- Salt and black pepper to taste

- ½ cup dried tarragon

- 1 tbsp 0% fat Greek yogurt

Directions:

1. Preheat the Air Fryer to 390° F. Lay out a 12 X 12 inch cut of foil on a flat surface. Place the chicken breasts on the foil, sprinkle the tarragon on both, and share the yogurt onto both breasts. Sprinkle with salt and pepper.

2. Loosely wrap the foil around the breasts to enable air flow. Place the wrapped chicken in the basket and cook for 12 minutes. Remove the chicken and carefully unwrap the foil. Serve with the sauce extract and steamed veggies.

Nutrition: Calories: 201 Fat: 4g Carbs: 9g Protein: 27g

Fruity Chicken Breasts with BBQ Sauce

Preparation Time: 10 minutes

Cooking time: 20 minutes

Servings: 2

Ingredients:

- 2 large chicken breasts, cubed

- 2 green bell peppers, sliced

- ½ onion, sliced

- 1 can drain pineapple chunks

- ½ cup low sugar barbecue sauce

Directions:

1. Preheat the Air Fryer to 370° F.

2. Thread the green bell peppers, the chicken, the onions and the pineapple chunks on the skewers.

3. Brush with barbecue sauce and fry for 20 minutes, until thoroughly cooked and slightly crispy.

Nutrition: Calories: 255 Fat: 4g Carbs: 9g Protein: 32g

Classic Chicken with Peanuts

Preparation Time: 10 minutes

Cooking time: 15 minutes

Servings: 4

Ingredients:

- 1 ½ pounds chicken tenderloins

- 2 tablespoons peanut oil

- 1/2 cup low fat parmesan cheese, grated

- Sea salt and ground black pepper, to taste

- 1/2 teaspoon garlic powder

- 1 teaspoon red pepper flakes

- 2 tablespoons peanuts, roasted and roughly chopped

Directions:

1. Start by preheating your Air Fryer to 360 ° F.

2. Brush the chicken tenderloins with peanut oil on all sides.

3. In a mixing bowl, thoroughly combine grated parmesan cheese, salt, black pepper, garlic powder, and red pepper flakes. Dredge the chicken in the breading, shaking off any residual coating.

4. Lay the chicken tenderloins into the cooking basket. Cook for 12 to 13 minutes or until it is no longer pink in the center. Work in batches; an instant-read thermometer should read at least 165° F.

5. Serve garnished with roasted peanuts. Bon appétit!

Nutrition: 354 Calories; 14g Fat; 3g Carbs; 40g Protein; 4g Sugars; 7g Fiber

Cod steaks with plum sauce

Preparation time: 10 minutes

Cooking time: 20 minutes

Servings: 2

Ingredients:

- 2 big cod steaks

- Salt and black pepper to the taste

- ½ teaspoon garlic powder

- ½ teaspoon ginger powder

- ¼ teaspoon turmeric powder

- 1 tablespoon low sugar plum sauce

- Cooking spray

Directions:

1. Season cod steaks with salt and pepper, spray them with cooking oil, add garlic powder, ginger powder and turmeric powder and rub well.

2. Place cod steaks in your air fryer and cook at 360 ° f for 15 minutes, flipping them after 7 minutes.

3. Heat a pan over medium heat, add plum sauce, stir and cook for 2 minutes.

4. Divide cod steaks on plates, drizzle plum sauce all over and serve.

5. Enjoy!

Nutrition: calories 250, fat 7, fiber 1, carbs 14, protein 12

Cod fillets and peas

Preparation time: 10 minutes

Cooking time: 10 minutes

Servings: 4

Ingredients:

- 4 cod fillets, boneless

- 2 tablespoons parsley, chopped

- 2 cups peas

- 4 tablespoons wine

- ½ teaspoon oregano, dried

- ½ teaspoon sweet paprika

- 2 garlic cloves, minced

- Salt and pepper to the taste

Directions:

1. In your food processor mix garlic with parsley, salt, pepper, oregano, paprika, and wine, blend well.

2. Rub fish with half of this mix, place in your air fryer and cook at 360 ° f for 10 minutes.

3. Meanwhile, put peas in a pot, add water to cover, add salt, bring to a boil over medium high heat.

4. Cook for 10 minutes, drain and divide among plates.

5. Also divide fish on plates, spread the rest of the herb dressing all over and serve.

6. Enjoy!

Nutrition: calories 261, fat 8, fiber 12, carbs 20, protein 22

Coconut coated fish cakes with mango sauce

Preparation: 20 minutes

Cooking time: 14 minutes

Servings: 4

Ingredients:

- 18 ounces of white fish fillet

- 1 green onion, finely chopped

- 1 mango, peeled, cubed

- 4 tablespoons of ground coconut

- 1½ ounces of parsley, finely chopped

- 1½ teaspoons of ground fresh red chili

- 1 lime, juice and zest

- 1 egg

- 1 teaspoon of salt

Directions:

1. Add ½ ounce of parsley, ½ teaspoon of ground chili, half of the lime juice and zest to the mango cubes and mix thoroughly.

2. Using a food processor, puree the fish and add the salt, egg, and lime zest, lime juice and chili. Stir in the green onions, 2 tablespoons of coconut and the rest of the parsley.

3. Put the rest of the coconut in a shallow dish. Mold the fish mixture into 12 round cakes. Place the cakes in the coconut to coat them.

4. Put half of the cakes into the fryer basket and bake for 7 minutes at 356°f. Remove when cakes are golden and bake the second batch of cakes.

5. Serve the cakes with the mango salsa.

Nutrition: Calories: 200 Fat: 13g Carbs: 8g Protein: 14g

Mango shrimp skewers

Preparation Time: 10 minutes

Cooking Time: 15 minutes

Servings:4

Ingredients:

- 2 tbsp olive oil

- ½ tsp garlic powder

- 1 tsp dry mango powder

- 2 tbsp fresh lime juice

- salt and black pepper to taste

Directions:

1. In a bowl, mix well the garlic powder, mango powder, lime juice, salt, and pepper. Add the shrimp and toss to coat. Cover and allow to marinate for minutes.

2. Preheat your Air Fryer to 390° F. Spray the air fryer basket with cooking spray.

3. Transfer the marinated shrimp to the cooking basket and drizzle the olive oil.

4. Cook for 5 minutes, Slide out the fryer basket and shake the shrimp; cook for 5 minutes.

5. Cool for 5 minutes and serve.

Nutrition: Calories: 261 Fat: 8g Carbs: 0g Protein: 28g

Fried Crawfish

Preparation Time: 5 minutes

Cooking Time: 5 minutes

Servings: 4

Ingredients:

- 1pound crawfish

- 1 tablespoon avocado oil

- 1 teaspoon onion powder

- 1 tablespoon rosemary, chopped

Directions:

1. Preheat the air fryer to 340°F.

2. Place the crawfish in the air fryer basket and sprinkle with avocado oil and rosemary. Add the onion powder and stir the crawfish gently.

3. Cook the meal for 5 minutes.

Nutrition: Calories: 370 Fat: 21g Carbs: 27g Protein: 17g

Sesame soy striped bass

Preparation time: 15 minutes

Cooking time: 10 minutes

Servings: 4

Ingredients:

- 1-pound striped bass steaks

- 1 cup soy sauce

- ½ cup mirin

- 2 tablespoons sesame oil

- 1 tablespoons brown sugar

- 1 tablespoon lime juice

- 1 tablespoon garlic chili paste

- ¼ cup apple juice

Directions:

1. Place the bass steaks in a shallow baking dish.

2. In a bowl, combine the soy sauce, mirin, sesame oil, brown sugar, lime juice, garlic chili paste, and apple juice. Use a whisk to blend.

3. Cover the steaks with the sesame soy sauce, cover, and refrigerate for one hour.

4. Set the air fryer to 390°f.

5. Remove the bass from the marinade and blot up any extra.

6. Place the steaks in the air fryer and cook for approximately 10 minutes, or until the fish is cooked through and flakey.

7. Remove the bass from the air fryer and let it rest several minutes before serving.

Nutrition: Calories 310, Total fat 12 g, Saturated fat 7 g, total carbohydrate 21 g, Dietary fiber 5 g, Sugars 13 g, protein 28 g

Fish and seafood recipes

Preparation time: 25 minutes

Cooking time: 20 minutes servings: 4

Ingredients:

- ½ pounds jumbo shrimp, cleaned, shelled and deveined

- 1-pound cherry tomatoes

- Tablespoons 0% fat yogurt

- 1 tablespoons sriracha sauce

- Sea salt and ground black pepper, to taste

- 1/2 teaspoon dried oregano

- 1/2 teaspoon dried basil

- 1 teaspoon dried parsley flakes

- 1/2 teaspoon marjoram

- 1/2 teaspoon mustard seeds

Directions

1. Toss all ingredients in a mixing bowl until the shrimp and tomatoes are covered on all sides.

2. Soak the wooden skewers in water for 15 minutes.

3. Thread the jumbo shrimp and cherry tomatoes onto skewers. Cook in the preheated air fryer at 400 ° f for 5 minutes, working with batches.

Nutrition: 247 calories; 4g fat; 6g carbs; 34g protein; 5g sugars; 8g fiber

Sesame nuggets

Preparation time: 15 minutes

Cooking time: 12 minutes

Servings: 6

Ingredients:

- 1 lb. chicken, cubed

- pinch sea salt

- 1 tsp sesame oil

- ¼ cup coconut flour

- ½ tsp ground ginger

- 4 egg whites

- 6 tbsp toasted sesame seeds

- cooking spray of choice

Directions:

1. Let your air fryer preheat to 400° f.

2. Meanwhile, toss the chicken cubes with sesame oil and salt.

3. Mix coconut flour with ground ginger in a Ziploc bag then place the chicken in it.

4. Zip the bag and shake well to coat the chicken well.

5. Whisk egg whites in a bowl then dip the coated chicken in egg whites.

6. Coat them with sesame seeds and shake off the excess.

7. Place the nuggets in the air fryer basket and return the basket to the fryer.

8. Air fry the nuggets for 6 minutes then flip them.

9. Spray the nuggets with cooking oil and cook for another 6 minutes.

10. Serve fresh.

Nutrition: calories 130 total fat 13 g saturated fat 4 g cholesterol 173 mg total carbs 9 g fiber 1 g sugar 2 g protein 77 g

Popcorn chicken

Preparation time: 2 hours

Cooking time: 8 minutes

Servings: 10

Ingredients:

- Marinade

- 2 lbs. chicken breast tenders, diced

- 2 cups almond milk

- 1 tsp salt

- ½ tsp black pepper

- ½ tsp ground paprika

- Dry ingredients

- 3 cups almond flour

- 3 tsp salt

- 2 tsp black pepper

- 2 tsp paprika

- oil spray

Directions:

1. Add all the ingredients for the marinade in a Ziplock bag.

2. Place the chicken in it then zip the bag. Shake it well then refrigerate for 2 hours or more.

3. Meanwhile, mix all the dry ingredients in a shallow container.

4. Remove the chicken from the marinade and dredge the pieces through the dry mixture.

5. Shake off the excess then place the pieces in the air fryer basket.

6. Spray them with cooking oil then return the basket to the air fryer.

7. Air fry them for 8 minutes at 370°f and toss them when cooked halfway through.

8. Serve immediately.

Nutrition: calories 242 total fat 19 g saturated fat 16 g cholesterol 36 mg total carbs 6 g fiber 2 g sugar 6 g protein 28 g

Breaded mushrooms

Preparation time: 15 minutes

Cooking time: 7 minutes

Servings: 2

Ingredients:

- ½ lb. button mushrooms

- 1 cup almond flour

- 1 egg

- 1 cup almond meal

- 3 oz grated low fat Parmigiano Reggiano cheese

- salt and pepper, to taste

Directions:

1. Let your air fryer preheat to 360° f.

2. Toss almond meal with cheese in a shallow bowl.

3. Whisk egg in one bowl and spread flour in another.

4. Wash mushrooms then pat dry. Coat each mushroom with flour.

5. Dip each of them in the egg then finally in the breadcrumbs mixture.

6. Shake off the excess and place the mushrooms in the air fryer basket.

7. Spray them with cooking oil and return the basket to the fryer.

8. Air fry these mushrooms for 7 minutes in the preheated air fryer.

9. Toss the mushrooms once cooked halfway through then continue cooking.

10. Serve warm.

Nutrition: calories 140 total fat 2 g saturated fat 2 g cholesterol 82 mg total carbs 9 g fiber 6 g sugar 1 g protein 3 g

Greek Meatballs with Feta

Preparation Time: 10 minutes

Cooking Time: 10 minutes

Servings: 2

Ingredients

- ½ pound ground beef
- 1 slice white bread, crumbled
- ¼ cup low fat feta cheese, crumbled
- 1 tablespoon fresh oregano, chopped
- 1 tablespoon fresh parsley, chopped
- ½ teaspoon ground black pepper
- A pinch of salt

Directions

1. In the large mixing bowl combine ground beef, breadcrumbs, fresh herbs, ground pepper and salt. Mix well to receive smooth paste.

2. Divide the mixture into 8-10 equal pieces.

3. Wet your hands and roll meatballs.

4. Preheat the Air Fryer to 370-390°F

5. Place meatballs into the Fryer and cook for 8-10 minutes, depending on the size of your meatballs.

6. Serve with rice or pasta.

Nutrition: Calories: 294 Fat: 11g Carbs: 26g Protein: 23g

Lemon sole and swiss chard

Preparation time: 10 minutes

Cooking time: 14 minutes

Servings: 4

Ingredients:

- 1 teaspoon lemon zest, grated
- 4 whole wheat bread slices, quartered
- ¼ cup walnuts, chopped
- ¼ cup low fat parmesan, grated
- 4 tablespoons olive oil
- 4 sole fillets, boneless
- Salt and black pepper to the taste
- 4 tablespoons 0% fat Greek Yogurt
- ¼ cup lemon juice
- 3 tablespoons capers
- 2 garlic cloves, minced
- 2 bunches swiss chard, chopped

Directions:

1. In your food processor, mix bread with walnuts, cheese and lemon zest and pulse well.

2. Add half of the olive oil, pulse well again and leave aside for now.

3. Heat up a pan with the yogurt over medium heat, add lemon juice, salt, pepper and capers, stir well, add fish and toss it.

4. Transfer fish to your preheated air fryer's basket, top with bread mix you've made at the beginning and cook at 350° f for 14 minutes.

5. Meanwhile, heat up another pan with the rest of the oil, add garlic, swiss chard, salt and pepper, stir gently, cook for 2 minutes and take off heat.

6. Divide fish on plates and serve with sautéed chard on the side.

7. Enjoy!

Nutrition: calories 321, fat 7, fiber 18, carbs 27, protein 12

Prawn Burgers

Preparation Time: 10 minutes

Cooking Time: 6 minutes

Servings: 2

Ingredients:

- ½ cup prawns, peeled, deveined and finely chopped
- ½ cup whole wheat breadcrumbs
- 23 tablespoons onion, finely chopped
- 3 cups fresh baby greens
- ½ teaspoon ginger, minced
- ½ teaspoon garlic, minced
- ½ teaspoon red chili powder
- ½ teaspoon ground cumin
- ¼ teaspoon ground turmeric
- Salt and ground black pepper, as required

Directions:

1. Preheat the Air fryer to 390° F and grease an Air fryer basket.
2. Mix the prawns, breadcrumbs, onion, ginger, garlic, and spices in a bowl.
3. Make small sized patties from the mixture and transfer to the Air fryer basket.

4. Cook for about 6 minutes and dish out in a platter.

5. Serve immediately warm alongside the baby greens.

Nutrition: Calories: 184 Fat: 3g Carbs: 13g Protein: 26g

Sardine Cakes

Preparation Time: 5 minutes

Cooking Time: 10 minutes

Servings: 5

Ingredients:

- 12 oz sardines, trimmed, cleaned

- ¼ cup coconut flour

- 1 egg, beaten

- 2 tablespoons flax meal

- 1 teaspoon ground black pepper

- 1 teaspoon salt

- Cooking spray

Directions:

1. Chop the sardines roughly and put them in the bowl. Add coconut flour, egg, flax meal, ground black pepper, and salt.

2. Mix up the mixture with the help of the fork. Then make 5 cakes from the sardine mixture.

3. Preheat the air fryer to 390°F. Add cooking spray to the air fryer basket and place the cakes inside.

4. Cook them for 5 minutes from each side.

Nutrition: Calories: 24 Carbs: 2g Protein: 1g

Mahi-mahi And Broccoli Cakes

Preparation Time: 5 minutes

Cooking Time: 11 minutes

Servings: 4

Ingredients:

- ½ cup broccoli, shredded

- 1 tablespoon flax meal

- 1 egg, beaten

- 1 teaspoon ground coriander

- 1 oz low fat Monterey Jack cheese, shredded

- ½ teaspoon salt

- 6 oz Mahi-mahi, chopped

- Cooking spray

Directions:

1. In the mixing bowl mix up flax meal, egg, ground coriander, salt, broccoli, and chopped Mahi-mahi.

2. Stir the ingredients gently with the help of the fork and add shredded Monterey Jack cheese. Stir the mixture until homogenous.

3. Then make 4 cakes. Preheat the air fryer to 390°F. Place the Mahi-mahi cakes in the air fryer and spray them gently with cooking spray.

4. Cook the fish cakes for 5 minutes and then flip on another side. Cook the fish cakes for 6 minutes more.

Nutrition: Calories: 150 Fat: 7g Carbs: 9g Protein: 13g

Tuna Au Gratin With Herbs

Preparation Time: 10 minutes

Cooking Time: 20 minutes

Servings: 4

Ingredients:

- 1 tablespoon 0% fat Greek Yogurt

- 1 medium sized leek, thinly sliced

- 1 tablespoon chicken stock

- 1 tablespoon dry white wine

- 1-pound tuna

- 1/2 teaspoon red pepper flakes, crushed

- Sea salt

- ground black pepper, to taste

- 1/2 teaspoon dried rosemary

- 1/2 teaspoon dried basil

- 1/2 teaspoon dried thyme

- 2 small ripe tomatoes, pureed

- 1 cup low fat Parmesan cheese, grated

Directions:

1. Melt 2 tablespoon of yogurt in a sauté pan over medium heat.

2. Now, cook the leek and garlic until tender and aromatic.

3. Add the stock and wine to deglaze the pan.

4. Preheat the Air Fryer to 370° F.

5. Grease a casserole dish with the remaining 1/2 tablespoon of melted butter. Place the fish in the casserole dish. Add the seasonings. Top with the sautéed leek mixture.

6. Add the tomato puree. Cook for 10 minutes in the preheated Air Fryer.

7. Top with grated Parmesan cheese; cook an additional 7 minutes until the crumbs are golden. Bon appétit!

Nutrition: Calories: 240 Fat: 1g Carbs: 30g Protein: 4g

Shrimp And Pine Nuts Mix

Preparation Time: 5 minutes

Cooking Time: 12 minutes

Servings: 4

Ingredients:

- ½ cup parsley leaves

- ½ cup basil leaves

- 2 tablespoons lemon juice

- 1/3 cup pine nuts

- ¼ cup low fat parmesan, grated

- A pinch of salt and black pepper

- ½ cup olive oil

- 1 and ½ pounds shrimp, peeled and deveined

- ¼ teaspoon lemon zest, grated

Directions:

1. Prepare all ingredients except the shrimp in blender and pulse well.

2. In a bowl, mix the shrimp with the pesto and toss.

3. Put the shrimp in your air fryer's basket and cook at 360° F for minutes, flipping the shrimp halfway.

4. Divide the shrimp into bowls and serve.

Nutrition: Calories: 365 Fat: 21g Carbs: 0g Protein: 0g

Garlic tarragon buttered salmon

Preparation time: 30 minutes

Cooking time: 20 minutes

Servings: 4

Ingredients:

- ¼ cup 0% fat Greek Yogurt

- 1 tablespoon shallot, diced

- 1 tablespoon fresh tarragon, chopped

- 1 teaspoon fresh lemon zest

- 1-pound salmon fillets

- 1 teaspoon salt

- 1 teaspoon black pepper

- Fresh lemon slices for garnish

Directions:

1. Set the air fryer to 350°f.

2. Melt the butter in a saucepan over medium heat.

3. Once the yogurt has melted, add the shallot, tarragon, and lemon zest. Cook, stirring frequently, for 2-3 minutes. Remove it from the heat and set it aside.

4. Season the salmon fillets with salt and black pepper.

5. Liberally brush both sides of each piece of salmon with the garlic tarragon butter.

6. Place the salmon pieces in the air fryer and cook for 15 minutes, turning once halfway through.

7. Remove the salmon from the air fryer and garnish with any remaining butter sauce and fresh lemon slices.

Nutrition: Calories 276, Total fat 15 g, Saturated fat 1 g, Total carbohydrate 4 g, dietary fiber 0 g, Sugars 0 g, Protein 21 g

Crumbed fish fillets with tarragon

Preparation time: 25 minutes

Cooking time: 20 minutes servings: 4

Ingredients:

- 2 eggs, beaten

- 1/2 teaspoon tarragon

- 4 fish fillets, halved

- 2 tablespoons dry white wine

- 1/3 cup low fat parmesan cheese, grated

- Teaspoon seasoned salt

- 1/3 teaspoon mixed peppercorns

- 1/2 teaspoon fennel seed

Directions

1. Add the parmesan cheese, salt, peppercorns, fennel seeds, and tarragon to your food processor; blitz for about 20 seconds.

2. Drizzle fish fillets with dry white wine. Dump the egg into a shallow dish.

3. Now, coat the fish fillets with the beaten egg on all sides; then, coat them with the seasoned cracker mix.

4. Air-fry at 345° f for about 17 minutes.

Nutrition: 305 calories; 17g fat; 3g carbs; 22g protein; 3g sugars; 1g fiber

Smoked and creamed white fish

Preparation time: 20 minutes

Cooking time: 15 minutes servings: 4

Ingredients:

- 1/2 tablespoon 0% fat yogurt

- 1/3 cup spring garlic, finely chopped

- Fresh chopped chives, for garnish

- 3 eggs, beaten

- 1/2 teaspoon dried dill weed

- Teaspoon dried rosemary

- 1/3 cup scallions, chopped

- 1/3 cup smoked whitefish, chopped

- 1 ½ tablespoon low fat crème fraiche

- 1 teaspoon kosher salt

- 1 teaspoon dried marjoram

- 1/3 teaspoon ground black pepper, or more to taste

- Cooking spray

Directions

1. Firstly, spritz four oven-safe ramekins with cooking spray. Then, divide smoked whitefish, spring garlic, and scallions among greased ramekins.

2. Crack an egg into each ramekin; add the crème, yogurt, and all seasonings.

3. Now, air-fry approximately 13 minutes at 355° f. Taste for doneness and eat warm garnished with fresh chives.

Nutrition: 249 calories; 21g fat; 6g carbs; 3g protein; 1g sugars; 7g fiber

Fish and cauliflower cakes

Preparation time: 2 hours 20 minutes

Cooking time: 13 minutes

Servings: 4

Ingredients:

- 1/2-pound cauliflower florets

- 1/2 teaspoon English mustard

- 2 tablespoons 0% fat Greek Yogurt

- 1/2 tablespoon cilantro, minced

- 2 tablespoons low fat sour cream

- 2 ½ cups cooked white fish

- Salt and freshly cracked black pepper, to savor

Directions

1. Boil the cauliflower until tender. Then, purée the cauliflower in your blender. Transfer to a mixing dish.

2. Now, stir in the fish, cilantro, salt, and black pepper.

3. Add the sour cream, English mustard, and butter; mix until everything's well incorporated. Using your hands, shape into patties.

4. Place in the refrigerator for about 2 hours. Cook for 13 minutes at 395° f. Serve with some extra English mustard.

Nutrition: 285 calories; 11g fat; 3g carbs; 31g protein; 6g sugars; 3g fiber

Grilled salmon with butter and wine

Preparation time: 45 minutes

Cooking time: 10 minutes servings: 4

Ingredients:

- 2 cloves garlic, minced

- 4 tablespoons 0% fat Greek Yogurt

- Sea salt and ground black pepper, to taste

- Teaspoon smoked paprika

- 1/2 teaspoon onion powder

- 1 tablespoon lime juice

- 1/4 cup dry white wine

- 4 salmon steaks

Directions

1. Place all ingredients in a large ceramic dish. Cover and let it marinate for 30 minutes in the refrigerator.

2. Arrange the salmon steaks on the grill pan. Bake at 390° for 5 minutes, or until the salmon steaks are easily flaked with a fork.

3. Flip the fish steaks, baste with the reserved marinade, and cook another 5 minutes.

Nutrition: 516 calories; 26g fat; 4g carbs; 67g protein; 7g sugars; 5g fiber

Mouth Watering Pork Tenderloin with Bell Pepper

Preparation Time: 7 minutes

Cooking Time: 15 minutes

Servings: 3

Ingredients

- 1-pound pork tenderloin

- 2 medium-sized yellow or red bell peppers, cut into strips

- 1 little onion, sliced

- 2 teaspoons Provencal herbs

- Salt and black pepper to taste

- 1 tablespoon olive oil

Directions

1. In the large mixing bowl combine sliced bell peppers, onions, and Provencal herbs. Season with salt and pepper to taste. Sprinkle with the olive oil and set aside.

2. Cut the pork tenderloin into 1-inch cubes and rub with salt and black pepper.

3. Preheat the air fryer to 370° F.

4. On the bottom of the air fryer basket lay seasoned meat and coat with vegetable mixture. Fry for 15 minutes, turning the meat and veggies once while cooking.

5. Serve with mashed potatoes.

Nutrition: Calories: 140 Fat: 6g Carbs: 3g Protein: 19g

Ground Beef

Preparation Time: 6 minutes

Cooking Time: 14 minutes

Servings: 3

Ingredients

- 2 tablespoons olive oil

- 1 medium onion, chopped

- 1-pound ground beef

- 1 bunch fresh spinach

- Salt and black pepper, to taste

Directions

1. Grease the baking tray with the olive oil.

2. Preheat the air fryer to 330° F. Add chopped onion to the tray and cook in the fryer for 2-3 minutes, stirring often. Add ground beef, mix well and cook for another 10 minutes, stirring occasionally.

3. Add chopped spinach, season with salt and pepper, stir to combine. Cook for 2-4 minutes until ready.

4. Serve and enjoy!

Nutrition: Calories: 231 Fat: 15g Carbs: 0g Protein: 23g

Rolled Up Tender Beef

Preparation Time: 10 minutes

Cooking Time: 20 minutes

Servings: 4

Ingredients

- 2-pound beef steak

- 5-6 slices low fat Cheddar cheese

- ½ cup fresh baby spinach

- 4 tablespoons Pesto

- 2 tablespoons 0%fat yogurt

- 1 teaspoon salt

- ¼ teaspoon black pepper

- 1 tablespoon olive oil

Directions

1. Open beef steak and spread the yogurt over the meat. Then cover it with pesto.

2. Layer cheese slices, baby spinach and season with salt and pepper. Roll up the meat and secure with toothpicks. Season with salt and pepper again.

3. Preheat the air fryer to 390° F and sprinkle frying basket with olive oil.

4. Place beef roll in the air fryer and cook for 15-20 minutes, turning couple times to roast from all sides.

5. Slice beef roll and serve with mashed potatoes or steamed rice.

Nutrition: Calories: 187 Fat: 8g Carbs: 16g Protein: 14g

& GREEN

Cinnamon butternut squash fries

Preparation time: 10 minutes

Cooking time: 10 minutes

Servings: 2

Ingredients:

- 1 pinch of salt

- 1 tbsp. Powdered unprocessed sugar

- ½tsp. Nutmeg

- 2 tsp. Cinnamon

- 1 tbsp. olive oil

- 10 ounces precut butternut squash fries

Directions:

1. In a plastic bag, pour in all ingredients. Coat fries with other components till coated and sugar is dissolved.

2. Spread coated fries into a single layer in the air fryer. Cook 10 minutes at 390°f until crispy.

Nutrition: calories: 175 fat: 8g protein: 1g sugar: 5g

Cheesy artichokes

Preparation time: 10 minutes

Cooking time: 14 minutes

Servings: 4

Ingredients:

- 4 artichokes, trimmed and halved

- 1 cup low fat cheddar cheese, shredded

- 2 tablespoons olive oil

- A pinch of salt and black pepper

- 3 garlic cloves, minced

- 1 teaspoon garlic powder

Directions:

1. In your air fryer's basket, combine the artichokes with the oil, cheese and the other ingredients, toss and cook at 400° f for 14 minutes.

2. Divide everything between plates and serve.

Nutrition: calories 191, fat 8, fiber 2, carbohydrates 12, protein 8

Paprika tomatoes

Preparation time: 10 minutes

Cooking time: 15 minutes

Servings: 4

Ingredients:

- 1pound cherry tomatoes, halved

- 1 tablespoon sweet paprika

- 2 tablespoons olive oil

- 2 garlic cloves, minced

- 1 tablespoon lime juice

- 1 tablespoon chives, chopped

Directions:

1. In your air fryer's basket, combine the tomatoes with the paprika and the other ingredients, toss and cook at a temperature of 370° f for 15 minutes.

2. Divide between plates and serve.

Nutrition: calories 131, fat 4, fiber 7, carbohydrates 10, protein 8

Avocado and tomato salad

Preparation time: 10 minutes

Cooking time: 12 minutes

Servings: 4

Ingredients:

- 1pound tomatoes, cut into wedges

- 2 avocados, peeled, pitted and sliced

- 2 tablespoons avocado oil

- 1 red onion, sliced

- 1 tablespoon balsamic vinegar

- Salt and black pepper to the taste

- 1 tablespoon cilantro, chopped

Directions:

1. In your air fryer, combine the tomatoes with the avocados and the other ingredients, toss and cook at 360° f for 12 minutes.

2. Divide between plates and serve.

Nutrition: calories 144, fat 7, fiber 5, carbohydrates 8, protein 6

Sesame broccoli mix

Preparation time: 5 minutes

Cooking time: 14 minutes

Servings: 4

Ingredients:

- 1pound broccoli florets

- 1 tablespoon sesame oil

- 1 teaspoon sesame seeds, toasted

- 1 red onion, sliced

- 1 tablespoon lime juice

- 1 teaspoon chili powder

- Salt and black pepper to the taste

Directions:

1. In your air fryer, combine the broccoli with the oil, sesame seeds and the other ingredients, toss and cook at 380° f for 14 minutes.

2. Divide between plates and serve.

Nutrition: calories 141, fat 3, fiber 4, carbohydrates 4, protein 2

Cabbage sauté

Preparation time: 5 minutes

Cooking time: 15 minutes

Servings: 4

Ingredients:

- 1pound red cabbage, shredded

- 1 tablespoon balsamic vinegar

- 2 red onions, sliced

- 1 tablespoon olive oil

- 1 tablespoon dill, chopped

- Salt and black pepper to the taste

Directions:

1. Heat up air fryer with oil at 380° f, add the cabbage, onions and the other ingredients, toss and cook for 15 minutes.

2. Divide between plates and serve.

Nutrition: calories 100, fat 4, fiber 2, carbohydrates 7, protein 2

Tomatoes and kidney beans

Preparation time: 10 minutes

Cooking time: 20 minutes

Servings: 4

Ingredients:

- 1pound cherry tomatoes, halved

- 1 cup canned kidney beans, drained

- 2 tablespoons balsamic vinegar

- 2 tablespoons olive oil

- 3 garlic cloves, minced

- Salt and black pepper to the taste

- 1 tablespoon chives, chopped

Directions:

1. In your air fryer, combine the cherry tomatoes with the beans and the other ingredients, toss and cook at 380° f for 20 minutes.

2. Divide between plates and serve.

Nutrition: calories 101, fat 3, fiber 3, carbohydrates 4, protein 2

Glazed mushrooms

Preparation time: 10 minutes

Cooking time: 15 minutes

Servings: 4

Ingredients:

- ½cup low sodium soy sauce

- 4 tablespoons fresh lemon juice

- 1 tablespoon maple syrup

- 4 garlic cloves, finely chopped

- Ground black pepper, as required

- 20 ounces fresh cremini mushrooms, halved

Directions:

1. Add the soy sauce, lemon juice, maple syrup, garlic and black pepper and mix well. Set aside.

2. Place the mushroom into the greased baking pan in a single layer.

3. Select "air fry" of digital air fryer oven and then adjust the temperature to 350° f.

4. Set the timer for 15 minutes and press "start/stop" to begin cooking.

5. When the unit beeps to show that it is preheated, insert the baking pan in the oven.

6. After 10 minutes of cooking, in the pan, add the soy sauce mixture and stir to combine.

7. When cooking time is complete, remove the mushrooms from oven and serve hot.

Nutrition: calories 70 total fat 3 g total carbohydrates 15 g protein 9 g

Balsamic zucchini slices

Preparation time: 5 minutes

Cooking time: 50 minutes

Servings: 6

Ingredients:

- 3 zucchinis, thinly sliced

- Salt and black pepper to taste

- 2 tablespoons avocado oil

- 2 tablespoons balsamic vinegar

Directions:

1. Add all the ingredients to a bowl and mix.

2. Put the zucchini mixture in your air fryer's basket and cook at 220° f for 50 minutes.

3. Serve as a snack and enjoy!

Nutrition: Calories 40 Fat 4 Fiber 2 Carbs 14 Protein 6

Turmeric carrot chips

Preparation time: 5 minutes

Cooking time: 25 minutes

Servings: 4

Ingredients:

- 4 carrots, thinly sliced

- Salt and black pepper to taste

- ½ teaspoon turmeric powder

- ½ teaspoon chat masala

- 1 teaspoon olive oil

Directions:

1. Place all ingredients in a bowl and toss well.

2. Put the mixture in your air fryer's basket and cook at 370° f for 25 minutes, shaking the fryer from time to time.

3. Serve as a snack.

Nutrition: Calories 161 Fat 4 fiber 2 carbs 14 protein 6

Conclusion

Thank you for reading all this book!

Anyone can make the recipes out of the air fryer. You need to know the right measurements, and you will have a great recipe ready for you. Once you know how to cook with an air fryer, you would want to cook in it every time. There are various recipes found in this book to try, so get started now without wasting any time!

You have already taken a step towards your improvement.

Best wishes!